BPD does not <u>define</u> me

By Elizabeth Schofield

I was born with a soul that is way too sensitive for this cold and ugly world, I have always felt things deeply and differently than most people. That has always been my blessing and my curse.

Reggie Nulan

Introduction

Borderline Personality Disorder or BPD is a mental health condition that affects 1.6% of the population with two thirds of those affected being women. BPD is also known as Emotionally Unstable Personality Disorder or EUPD. BPD is generally brought on by trauma, usually from childhood, and it affects a person's mood meaning their moods are heightened and the individual is more likely to cause harm to themselves or sometimes others.

I am diagnosed with BPD. I say diagnosed rather than I have because it is not a part of me, it is merely a diagnosis. I first experienced mental health issues when I was 14 years old, nearly 11 years ago. I started to self-harm after a traumatic incident and I also developed eating disorders. As well as this I developed agoraphobia, fear of leaving the house, and couldn't go to school for about 5 months which wasn't great as my GCSE's were coming up. I started going to CAMHS, a child and adolescent mental health service which helped for a while. At around 16, I started to hallucinate and become paranoid, but I kept this to myself. It was very scary as I didn't feel safe. I had started college at this point and my therapist at CAMHS came to a meeting with the college and said she didn't feel the therapy was helping me, so I was discharged from their care. I continued to self-harm which got worse as I perfected techniques.

It wasn't until I was 21 that my self-harming and hallucinations got so bad I had to be hospitalised. It was a fight to get me into hospital, but I wasn't safe so my dad and boyfriend at the time supported me in getting myself admitted. My boyfriend had taken videos of me self-harming and attempting suicide and I was saying that the hallucinations were making me do it. It was very scary, and I genuinely believed I had to die or the hallucinations would hurt my family. I also developed a delusion, that I was from another world and I believed I had to die in this world to be reborn in MY world, so I could lead my army into battle. It sounds silly writing it now but that is something I truly believed. When I was admitted into hospital 7 years after I started developing signs of mental illness which was when I was diagnosed with BPD and so my journey began.

I would describe BPD as a cross between autism and schizophrenia. This is because BPD means you find it difficult to regulate your emotions or understand other people's emotions. It is also like schizophrenia because you can hallucinate and have delusions, although people diagnosed with BPD generally hear voices in their head rather than externally. I also experience visual hallucinations which is uncommon and the voices I hear are attached to the person or animal I can see. I tend to see children or animals which are nice but there are also hallucinations that scare me and hurt me. I can physically feel pain in my body when I am being attacked by a hallucination, but everyone is different, and you may not experience this for yourself. Honestly, I hope you don't!

The symptoms of BPD vary for each person and you will not experience the same extremes as someone else. The symptoms of BPD are:

1. Fear of abandonment

2. Unstable relationships

3. Unclear or unstable self-image

4. Impulsive, self-destructive behaviours

5. Self-harm

6. Extreme mood swings

7. Chronic feelings of emptiness

8. Explosive anger

9. Feeling suspicious or out of touch with reality

I will attempt to make sense of these symptoms for you in the chapters to come. I will explain what they mean but also what they mean to me. I will write my own experiences of BPD, what it means to me and, also tell you my story as we go through the book. I hope that you find this book helpful whether you have been diagnosed with BPD yourself or are looking up what to expect from a loved one. It may also be useful to read if you are a health professional as BPD is generally misunderstood and used to diagnose someone with emotional issues and/or hallucinations where another diagnosis may fit. I know people who were first diagnosed with BPD but have since been diagnosed with another mental health condition such as bipolar or schizophrenia. BPD is generally not diagnosed on its own but comes with another diagnosis such as depression, bipolar or anxiety.

1. Fear of abandonment

Fear of abandonment is a real issue for people diagnosed with BPD. It tends to be more extreme than a typical fear and means that a person may end relationships through fear of them leaving. This fear usually stems from childhood abuse or neglect and means a person with BPD can get attached to other people easily.

My experience of fearing abandonment means I get attached to people and also push people away but when my condition was at its worst I would feel scared and upset when I was out shopping, and I lost sight of the person I was shopping with. This first happened when I went shopping with my dad when he came to visit me. When my illness got to its worst and I had been in hospital in England, my dad sent me to live in Wales with my mum. I had been sleeping rough when I was at my dad's and I was having hallucinations that told me to hurt my younger sister. She was getting ready to sit her GCSE's at the time and my dad worked full time so could not make sure I was safe. I did not want to move to Wales as my whole life, family and friends were in England, but my family couldn't see any other way. My mum did not work and could therefore look after me. I was in the car with the child lock on in case I got scared and tried to leave while my dad was driving on the motorway. I resented my family for forcing me to move but now I realise it was the best thing that could have happened to me because the metal health services in Wales were so much better than England.

When I first lived in Wales my dad would try and visit me often. I still had a strong feeling that I didn't want to be in Wales so when he visited I would get scared if he went out of my sight. I desperately wanted to go back to England and my mum hid by purse, so I couldn't buy a coach or train ticket. It seems extreme, like I was a prisoner, but who knew what would happen if I went off on my own. I love living in Wales now, after 3 years, and the scenery and beaches are amazing. I visit my family and friends every year, getting the coach to go see them but it wasn't always easy for me. When I first came to Wales I wouldn't go out the house without my mum because I feared getting lost and it wasn't until recently that I have been able to go shopping by myself.

I believe I first experience fear of abandonment when I was 14. It is one of the first issues I remember having but at the time it was taken as anxiety. I used to wait for my dad to come home from work, which was usually between 6 and 7pm but some nights he worked late or went shopping after work and him not being home by 7 or 8pm would lead me to think up horrible scenarios why he wasn't home, such as he had been involved in a car crash. I would try to phone him to see why he was late but if he was driving then he rightly wouldn't answer. I used to do a workshop with CAMHS on anxiety and I had a booklet that I filled in to say what I had been scared of, what I did and how I overcame it. I also wrote my eating disorder in this booklet, saying I had tried a new food and rewarded myself with a pudding I liked. I realise now that what I was experiencing wasn't anxiety and was in fact the warning signs of BPD but when you are still a child or adolescent, mental health services do not like to make rash diagnosis or give out medication.

Fear of abandonment is the first symptom of BPD as it is the fuel that leads to unstable relationships, poor self-image or changes in behaviour. If a person diagnosed with BPD feels they have been let down then they begin to feel that they are not good enough or are worthless, which leads them to behave in a radical way such as self-harm. It also affects a person's relationships as they can go from someone being the best person in the world to hating them. This is also characteristic of people diagnosed with BPD and means they can lose friendships or romantic relationships due to their perception of an individual being changed. A person with BPD is often described as seeing things in black and white, there is no grey. This means that people are often good or bad but never in between.

People diagnosed with BPD can also become attached to individuals, whether they are teachers, support workers or health professionals and this can be upsetting for the individual if they are discharged from the care of someone they like. I remember when I was discharged from hospital in Wales and the home treatment team, who make sure you are safe to be at home and settling back in, kept changing the person who was coming to see me and discharged me from their care early due to knowing that I could get attached to someone. I also struggle with change which is something I worked on with my psychologist and knowing I liked butterflies she printed out a quote for me which read 'If nothing ever changed, there would be no butterflies'.

A person diagnosed with BPD may display inappropriate anger if they are faced with a short- term separation or there are unavoidable changes in plans. This is because they feel that they are being abandoned or that they are not good enough for the other person. The symptoms of BPD are usually irrational but a person experiencing the illness will feel emotions intently and take what they see as rejection to heart. A person experiencing fear of abandonment will want to be with other people, not on their own, which can be why they struggle with people leaving or changing plans. A person diagnosed with BPD will latch on to others because they do not want to be alone. They tend to idealize the person they are latched on to, feeling that they are the best person and want to be around them all the time.

Personally, I often wonder what it would be like to be someone else, to experience someone else's emotions and live as they do. I also think about what I have said after it has come out of my mouth and wonder what other people are thinking of my conversation or actions. It can get very annoying as you cannot just have a conversation and think about what to say next, due to analysing your own sentence. I have got better at this recently and now I just say what is in my head. I also struggle with self-esteem and want to know what other people think of me. I struggle with making friends and don't understand when someone is a friend or simply a colleague. It is a lot friendlier in Wales than England though and I have found that I can say hello to people walking in the street.

Another issue with fear of abandonment is a friend having other friends that they spend time with as someone experiencing heightened fear will think that they are not good enough for their friend to spend with them and instead sees their friend's other friends as a threat. A person experiencing these extreme emotions will struggle with self-esteem and will want their friend to themselves rather than sharing them. This can lead to a break down in friendship or a romantic relationship because the individual will start to hate and distrust their friend or boyfriend/ girlfriend. This can make it difficult for a person diagnosed with BPD to make or keep relationships. The individual may also express impulsive or self-destructive behaviour due to the fear and anxiety surrounding what they see as a threat.

2. Unstable relationships

Unstable relationships mean the relationship you have with friends, family or a boy/girlfriend. With BPD you tend to feel emotions intensely which can lead to tension and heightened emotions towards someone you care about.

My first experience of unstable relationships was when I had made a new friend on a course I was completing. We started off close, talking to each other and having a laugh but after a while I started to lash out. I don't know why I did it, but I also lost friends when I went into hospital. I had two close friends who said they would come visit me if I was ever put into hospital, but they never did. I spoke to them at first when I moved away but the new friend stopped talking to me. I did see my other friend on a visit back to England when she told me she was pregnant but after she had her son we didn't talk anymore. I am happy to say though that an old school friend got back in touch and we see each other for dinner each time I go back to visit.

Another experience with unstable relationships was directed first came to light when I had a boyfriend and I would feel paranoid that he would cheat on me and I directed anger towards him. We would get into physical fights and it was unhealthy. Then when, as I explained in the previous chapter, I was forced to move away from home, I resented my dad for forcing me to leave. I directed a lot of anger towards my family for leaving me. I also felt anger towards my dad because when I first tried to tell him about my problems and showed him pictures I had drawn of the people and animals I see, he didn't react very well, and I am not sure he believed me. I know it must be hard to see a loved one unwell, but you should not tell someone who is having hallucinations or delusions that they are not real, or you don't believe them.

There was also a bit of tension between my dad and my boyfriend at the time because I only let my boyfriend see how I reacted to my hallucinations, he was the only one who knew I was seeing them. My boyfriend did try on several occasions to persuade me to tell my dad, but I didn't want him to know. My wishes were respected but my dad was not happy that he had not been told and my boyfriend was drained from dealing with it all on his own.

While I was living in Wales, my illness progressed, I couldn't sleep most nights and was thinking about self-harm and suicide constantly. I would try to talk to my boyfriend at the time when I was feeling low but that did mean I would phone him at 3am which he and his family were not pleased about. I was in hospital in Wales, on a high security ward, when I was sent back to England because I was still registered with my old GP. I was put into the local psychiatric hospital where I was displaying a lot of anger and practically sedated to keep me calm and ensure no one came to harm. The hospital discharged me, and I went into the woods nearby and stayed hidden for days with no food or water. I was eventually picked up by police when I collapsed and was found by a passer-by. My family and boyfriend had been looking for me and put up posters around the area and on Facebook. When I went back to Wales, my boyfriend split up with me, he couldn't deal with all the drama and that hurt.

I have since had trouble with relationships, I don't know if it's me or who I am choosing but they don't work out. My last man I was properly seeing was married with children but was separated from his wife. He is 5 years older than me, but we got on really well, could talk openly and I have experience working with children, so he knew I would be good with his. In the end the man decided to go back to his wife which was absolutely heart breaking as I hadn't realised that I had truly fallen for him. This has made it difficult for me to commit to men since and I end up pushing people away.

You may have different experiences with relationships, it may be with friends, family or a partner but whoever it is, don't blame yourself. Once you are on the right medication and getting the right support, you can work through any problems you have.

I thought that I would have a strained relationship with my mum as I didn't have the best childhood with her, but she has been so supportive and learned how to help me. My mum was diagnosed with post-natal depression after having my sister 19 years ago and takes an anti-depressant. This has really helped our relationship as I know that my mum understands what I am going through and is supportive, even if she doesn't fully understand psychosis. My mum has been on courses to help her better understand me and help with her own feeling, there is support out there for everyone who needs it and she has really tried to help me. She visited me when I was in hospital and we have a great relationship now. That is proof that you can overcome trauma, mental illness and distant relationships and help each other get through it.

I am not convinced that the symptoms of an illness such as BPD fully go away, they can be helped by medication and support, but I think you need to constantly work on how to deal with your emotions in a positive way. Mindfulness and activities such as art or music can really help a person express themselves. You will find other people who are going through or have been through a mental illness and it is good to talk openly about it and always say when you are struggling. Bottling up emotions will only lead them to come out in an explosive, negative way which is unhealthy.

I believe that there is the tendency to develop a mental illness in all of us and all it takes is for something to trigger it so be aware that people may be suffering and not tell you about it. Family is a great support and can help you through this time so if you or your loved one is struggling then please talk. There is nothing to be ashamed of, stigma and bias shame us all. You may not be able to retrieve a relationship or pick up where you left off, but it is important to take on board the experience to help you with any future relationships with friends or loved ones.

My final note to say on unstable relationships is that you should always put yourself first. It is not selfish, it is important to anyone's mental health that they look after themselves first and protect themselves from harm. Your emotions and wellbeing are more important. If you don't feel comfortable around someone then voice this or if you have to, cut ties with them. This may sound harsh, but it is better to have people around you that care about you and don't make you feel like you are any less important. Look after yourself and in turn you can look after others.

3. Unclear or unstable self-image

An unclear or unstable self-image refers to not knowing who you are or where you belong in the world. Having an unstable self-image in terms of BPD is sometimes called identity diffusion. It means that you do not know who you are, what your personality is or what defines you. It can also mean you feel lost and like you do not belong in the world. This can lead a person to self-harm or attempt suicide as they want to feel like someone else.

A stable self-image is being able to see yourself the same in the past, present and future and knowing who you are even if you behave in a way that contradicts this. A person may see themselves as kind and loving but lash out at a friend because they are being mean. A person with a stable self-image would be able see that it was situation that made them behave badly and know that they are still kind and loving. However, a person with an unstable self-image will look at themselves differently and start to think that they are a bad and mean person. They will not see that they behaved in this way as a reaction and would begin to look at themselves negatively and even try to live up to this new self-image.

Having a strong self-image can lead to good self-esteem and people thinking good of themselves. If someone is praised for good art work, then they gain confidence and increase their self-esteem levels. A person diagnosed with BPD who has an unstable self-image will not think good of themselves, they may think that they are receiving praise through pity which will mean they do not have good self-esteem. Having good self-esteem is important because it means that a person can grow in confidence and pursue their ambitions.

People diagnosed with BPD often do not follow their dreams because they do not think they are good enough or deserve it. I did not start a university degree until I was 22 because I used to think that I wasn't good enough for university and that I would struggle. After being unwell for so long and meeting lots of people such as occupational therapists and psychologists, who helped me over the years, I decided to study psychology with the open university. It is hard, but I am studying part time so am going at a steady pace and can still work. I now have a better self-image and self-esteem due to studying for 2 years and selling canvas paintings in a local shop. It is good to stick with hobbies that make you happy and it is a wonderful feeling when you know you have helped someone.

My experience of unstable self-image started in my teens, I did not know who I was, what defined me or what I wanted. I would often look at other people and wonder what it would be like to be them, which still happens to me sometimes. I often look at another person and want to have their personality traits such as confidence or posture. I also experienced this when I was struggling with eating disorders and would look at another girl and think 'I wish I had her legs'. Having an unstable self-image can be very difficult as it makes you feel you are not worthy as a person and you think others don't like you for you or would rather you have a different personality.

Having an unstable self-image can lead to a person putting on an act of confidence or trying to walk in a different way because they want to be seen differently and think others will like them better. Another part of mental illness can be a person mirroring. Mirroring means that you copy someone else's gestures or speech patterns which usually happens in a social situation. When I first went into hospital I was told that I was mirroring other people and my boyfriend at the time said it made him feel that he didn't really know who I was. I would mirror my friends' actions and be more confident and outgoing when I was around them. It is a hard diagnosis to have as you feel like you don't know where you start, and another person ends.

I would say that mirroring links to self-image because you mirror people when you are not comfortable or confident with who you are. It is a way of pretending to be someone else and makes you want what that person has. A person can be a mix of different friend's or family's traits, gestures and emotions which makes it very hard for someone diagnosed with BPD to know who they are. I also used to copy phrases and voices of people I watched on YouTube to feel what it would be like to be them.

It is not nice to feel like you do not belong in the world and can make you feel self-conscious and depressed. I used to cry and get frustrated with myself or even think about what I have said because I was worried the person I was talking to would take what I was saying in the wrong way. It is emotionally draining to constantly be thinking about what you are saying or how you are behaving and being worried or even paranoid that people do not like you or are talking about you.

I have learned to be myself, to act naturally and say what comes into my head even if I am angry or upset because it shows people how I am feeling. I can be snappy sometimes which is how my family know I may be becoming unwell again but it is important for them to see that, so they can help me. I also struggle with self-image in the sense of what I look like, so I exercise regularly and try to eat healthy. I think that side of self-image is important because if you look good then you feel good. I have struggled with my weight, putting on 3 stone in 2 years due to being on the anti-psychotic medication olanzapine. It made me feel self-conscious, but I was very slim to start with. I also got diagnosed with IBS and lactose intolerance a few months ago and I was so bloated that people asked if I was pregnant, including the GP! This made me aware of how I was looking, and I also became paranoid that people were talking about me. I have lost a stone since being diagnosed with IBS and exercising is great for your mental health as well as physical.

I have learned to love myself for who I am and so can you. There is nothing wrong with you and there are people who care about you. If you are a friend or family member of someone diagnosed with BPD, then please be patient and kind. Reassure your loved one that they are wonderful the way they are, and they do belong here. It can be hard to struggle with self-image and it does take time, but you will learn to be happy with who you are and realise that people do love you for you. While you are unwell you only see how you are affected and being admitted into hospital is not good for someone with BPD, so I would encourage you to reach out to friends and loved ones to reassure you and speak to your GP.

4. Impulsive, self-destructive behaviours

17

Impulsive behaviour manifests itself in different ways and is common in other mental illnesses such as bipolar. Impulsive behaviour can mean going on a shopping spree without worrying how much you are spending and can lead to debt or at the low end it can mean jeopardising relationships. Impulsive and self-destructive behaviours can be subconscious, meaning you don't realise you are doing them. You may push family or friends away because you feel that you don't deserve their love. A person in the depths of a mental illness will often say or do things they do not mean and can be unaware that they are harming themselves in this way.

My experience of impulsive behaviour is that when I was unwell I would become aggressive and emotionally manipulative, pushing people away through anger and emotional blackmail. I have been admitted to psychiatrist hospitals a lot over 2-year periods and when they do not have a bed locally but feel you need to be sectioned then they would send you to a hospital mile's away. I live in Wales but have been sent to hospitals in England due to there being no beds in my area. It was difficult to be away from family and not be able to have visitors. I feel this made my behaviour worse as I was isolated. Due to my illness I would try to emotionally blackmail my mum into visiting me or sending me my university books so that I could continue my studies. Luckily, the staff were good and let me use their computer to do my work

I also use self-destructive behaviour when I am unwell which does not necessarily mean self-harming but can mean isolating yourself from others and denying yourself to feel emotions. When I was unwell at home I would stay in my room all the time, only coming out to get food or drink. My mum would be sitting in the garden, in the dun, but I would feel that I had to cut myself off from everyone and deal with my illness alone. I would not leave the house at all and would just read a book or watch YouTube on my phone.

Denying yourself to grieve when a loved one has passed is also classed as self-destructive behaviour although you would not think it. I believe it is anyway. When my grandad passed away a couple of years ago I became unwell and had to go into a unit. There was a lovely nurse in the hospital who spoke to me about my grief and explained that I was in denial. I told her that I knew my grandad was dead, but she said I wasn't in denial of his death, but I was of my emotions, I wasn't allowing myself to grieve. I have to say that the staff in the hospital were very good to me and would comfort me when I cried. One student nurse even got me balloons so that I could write a message to my grandad and send it off into the sky. On the day of my grandad's funeral, staff let me stay in bed because they knew it was a difficult day for me. I am grateful to all the staff who have helped me to learn how to cope with my emotions and when my best friend passed in March 2018 I was able to deal with her death better and attend her funeral.

Self-destructive behaviour for those diagnosed with BPD can mean self-harm and suicidal behaviour which I will go into more in the next chapter. Self-harm can mean anything from cutting to burning, hair pulling and head banging. Three- quarters of those diagnosed with BPD will self-harm in some way. They may do it due to anger, frustration, as punishment, to feel something, for attention or to shift pain from mental to physical.

I have engaged in self harm since I was 14, nearly 11 years ago. I started off cutting but when I became unwell and was in hospital I would get so frustrated that I would head bang and started severely burning myself. I am covered in scars which does bother me sometimes, but I have learned to live with them and don't hide them anymore. I have also attempted to take my life a number of times through ligatures and drinking bleach. I would like to take this opportunity to tell you that it does not have to come to this, you are a precious member of society and everyone has something to offer. Find a way to deal with your anger and frustration in a more productive way such as exercise, art work or writing. I have found all of these things useful and because I struggle to express myself verbally, writing is a great way to get your feelings out. You do not have to share your work with anyone but use it as a way to express yourself. Everyone is different and therefore you will find your own way to express yourself.

Another type of impulsive and self-destructive behaviour is substance abuse. This can be drugs or alcohol and is used to drown out your emotions and difficulties. I have never taken drugs, and never will as they be dangerous and addictive. However, I have used alcohol to numb my pain before. When I first started to get paranoid and struggle with my feelings at 17, I decided to drown out the hallucinations through drinking a whole bottle of wine in 10 minutes. This was very dangerous and if I hadn't have thrown up then I could have died of alcohol poisoning. Alcohol and drugs are both used to help an individual deal with a mental illness, but it is not healthy.

Shoplifting is also a form of self-destructive behaviour as a person will get a rush of fear which makes them feel alive even if they are caught. Reckless driving is also used as a self-destructive behaviour and can be dangerous for the individual but also other drivers on the road. Reckless driving can be used to make someone feel alive but also as a way to end their suffering by attempting to take their own life if they drive into a lake, verge or another car at high speed. It is not a good idea to drive when you are angry or upset as it can be fatal to not only you, but other drivers and you may end up in prison.

A final form of self-destructive behaviour that I can relate to is binge eating. If a person is emotional due to a mental illness, then they may choose food to help them gain some control into their life. This can be done through starvation or binge eating. When a person binge eats, they are eating their emotions or stuffing them further down their body. A person may make themselves vomit or exercise excessively, known as purging, to get rid of the food that they have just eaten. Emotional eating is very common and both obesity and eating disorders are on the rise.

I first started to binge eat when I was a teenager after developing an eating disorder. I first starved myself but then the desire for food took over and I would binge and purge by vomiting to make sure I did not put on any weight. I struggled with eating disorders for several years and would binge and purge in secret. I also put on 3 stone in 2 years when I was put on olanzapine, an anti-psychotic, but I have decided to get the weight off healthily through a good diet and plenty of exercise. Exercise helps you to feel good as well as gives you energy. I would recommend exercising to anyone struggling with a mental illness but make sure that you eat enough too!

5. Self-harm

I touched on self-harm a bit on the previous chapter and its role in self-destructive behaviour. There are several forms of self-harm, but the most common forms are cutting and burning yourself. Other forms of self-harm include scratching, pinching, punching things and the less obvious making yourself sick.

I first starting self-harming when I was 14, cutting myself with scissors and moving on to burning myself. I have self-harmed a lot over the last 10 years and I used it as a way of letting out anger, punishing myself or asking for attention. I say that I used it to ask for attention, but it was not attention seeking as some people might think. I didn't know how to verbalise that I needed help like a lot of young people do not, so I used self-harm as a way of saying that something was wrong, and I needed help.

I did not start to severely self-harm until I had a psychotic episode that led to me being hospitalised. I self-harmed in an extreme way by burning myself with hot mugs which led to pouring boiling water on myself. My most severe scars are burns and I think they are the worst form of self-harm as they are painful and can lead to infections, especially if they are not doused in cold water. I am not saying that anyone should self-harm or trying to give tips, but I am telling you the forms of self-harmed used and that they are dangerous!

When I was admitted into a hospital in Wales I would self-harm and then pick the scabs and make them bleed. It was explained to me by a nurse that picking the scabs was a form of self-harm because even though I was not actually cutting or burning myself, I was trying to harm myself by making myself bleed and causing pain.

I would also say that suicide attempts can be a way of self-harming and crying out for help. A suicide attempt is a way of trying to end your life because you cannot cope anymore but it can also be used to make people notice how much you are struggling. Suicide attempts can also be extreme and very dangerous as you may end your life. I used to ligature a lot and pass out from not being able to breathe and an ambulance would have to be called. The first night I was in a psychiatric unit I ligatured and had to have oxygen. I have also caused myself to bleed through the nose and mouth from ligaturing, so it is very dangerous and a real cry for help! I have also drunk bleach in the past to try to end my life and have had to have a camera down my throat to assess the damage caused to my oesophagus. Again, I am only explaining my own experiences and am not giving tips, please do not try this as it is dangerous!

Self-harming can also mean making yourself sick if it is less about food and feeling fat and more about trying to harm your body. I first developed an eating disorder when I was 14 and a part of that was to make myself sick. Then, it was not a form of self-harm and as about control and getting rid of food I had binged on. Bulimia is a mental illness in its own right and you may have an eating disorder along with another mental illness, but I am going to concentrate on self-harming through making yourself sick for this book on BPD. Making yourself sick for self-harm reasons is less about food and more about causing yourself pain. The most common way to make yourself sick is to put something down your throat, such as your fingers or a toothbrush, in order to activate reflux. This is considered self-harm because you are deliberately causing yourself pain.

A less severe form of self-harming is to scratch or bite yourself, whether this causes bleeding or not. This is less common but is generally used by distressed children or adults who do not have other options. Any form of inflicting pain on yourself is classed as self-harm and self-harming can be hard to control when you are distressed or anxious. Symptoms of self-harm can be managed with medication and therapy, but the habit can be hard to break if you have been doing it for a long time.

Self-harming for those diagnosed with BPD can be different to a person who is diagnosed with depression. A characteristic of BPD is extreme mood swings and a person experiencing this may resort to self-harm to control these feelings. Severe mood swings can be extreme rage or sadness which means a person diagnosed with BPD can feel out of control and not know what to do for the best. Medication is a big factor for this illness as it is generally used to control mood swings. The first time I saw a psychiatrist in Wales he said that I went through about 10 different emotions in the space of an hour. I still get angry and upset but I take sertraline and olanzapine to help with low moods, as a mood stabiliser and an anti-psychotic. I will talk about extreme mood swings more in the next chapter but as you have probably noticed, all these symptoms link in to each other.

Self-harm often comes with negative image as people will think you are attention seeking. Over the years, especially at school, I have been bullied for my self-harming and had nasty comments from fellow students such as 'go slit your wrists, curl up and die'. I hope that this is not the case in schools now and that students are taught more about self-harm and how to help someone who is struggling. Self-harming also causes a lot of scarring and I have scars all over my body and severe burn marks on my arms from the years of pain I have put my body through. Self-harm scars made me self-conscious about my body and I wouldn't wear shorts or a bikini for a long time, but I have learned that I do not need to cover up, if someone else has a problem then that's their problem, not mine. I still struggle with self-confidence, but I have learned to ignore other people and be happy in myself. I hope you do too!

6. Extreme mood swings

Extreme mood swings are a common symptom of BPD and can be quite noticeable by other people. Extreme mood swings are not only categorised by 'negative' emotions such as anger or sadness but can be 'positive' emotions such as happiness. A person diagnosed with BPD can experience any mood within a short period of time and what makes it a symptom of this illness is the amount of time between moods. An average person may experience different moods throughout the day due to events, but a person diagnosed with BPD can experience several moods in a short space of time.

As I said in the last chapter, it was suspected that I was displaying symptoms of BPD because I went through several emotions in the space of an hour. This can be very draining for anyone as you do not know how you are going to feel from one minute to the next. I was also told that when I decided to stop my medication I was on a 'high', this is where you are extremely happy and can express this through dancing and being overjoyed by everything. This was a side effect of me not taking my medication and it did lead to me going depressed quite quickly, so I went back on my medication. I would not advise anyone to stop taking their medication unless they have consulted a doctor. You would think that extreme highs and lows are more likely to be symptoms of an illness such as bipolar, but anyone can get these symptoms.

Doctors and psychiatrists find it very difficult to diagnose a mental illness such as bipolar or schizophrenia, so they tend to say that a person has BPD as it's easier. Some psychiatrists do not believe in the diagnosis of BPD and I have been told by these professionals that they think it's an easy diagnosis to make when a person is presenting symptoms of mood swings, self-harm and psychosis.

I know people who were first diagnosed with Borderline Personality Disorder before their symptoms progressed into more like another illness such as bipolar. It is also claimed by some professionals that BPD is not life long and with the right medication and therapy a person can have the label removed. However, I have spoken to other professionals who believe it is not something you can stop through medication. When I see my diagnosis on forms, I often see different categories in my diagnosis. It is believed that psychosis is a symptom of BPD, but I have seen on forms that I am diagnosed with BPD, psychosis and depression rather than just BPD. This makes it very difficult to know what you are looking at as professionals have different opinions.

Extreme mood swings when you are diagnosed with BPD can change rapidly and you do not know how you are going to feel next. The extreme moods can be helped with medication such as mood stabilisers which are usually old drugs that were used to treat illnesses such as epilepsy. It is important that you work with your psychiatrist to find the right medication that works for you. Anti-psychotics can also be used to stabilise moods as well as help with hallucinations and delusions. You may also need to try an anti-depressant as this helps with low moods. I currently take sertraline for depression and olanzapine for mood and psychosis, but I did start off on risperidone for mood and psychosis, although I had to change it due to side effects such as restless legs and feel disconnected. Different medications work for different people as everyone's body and brain will respond in a different way.

Since I started taking medication about 3 years ago my moods swings have improved dramatically, however, I still get bouts of anger and frustration. I am no longer depressed but it is the anger that means I can snap at people and get annoyed easily. This is not a nice feeling to have but it isn't a mood that stays. Often, this anger is directed towards my mum because I live with her and we can clash and get under each other's feet. However, this has been better since I started working and now my mum is volunteering. I also attend exercise classes during the week which not only means that my mum and I get space from each other but exercise releases endorphins that make you feel happy. I also use my anger in these classes to work hard and get the best results for myself. I would highly recommend exercise as it helps improve your mood and allows you to interact with other people who do not need to know your struggles.

Mental illnesses cannot be discovered through blood tests and therefore it is important to talk about your symptoms with a professional. Talking is the best cure for mental illness as it means you can share how you are feeling and what you are thinking. It is also ok to cry or laugh, depending on how you are feeling. It is important to let out your emotions and not let them fester inside you until they burst. Extreme moods can show a person that you are struggling and get you the help you need. A way of expressing your pain is through inflicting physical pain on yourself or others. This is a sign that someone is struggling and needs you to support them. One person may self-harm to relieve their emotions, whereas someone else may deliberately get into fights or drink/ drugs. These are all signs to look out for and show that a person needs help and support.

Extreme mood swings are not the type of mood swing that a teenager may have due to hormones but are more severe and are usually more frequent. It is important to know the difference between an adolescent or even an adult showing signs of being in a mood and having extreme mood swings. A person having an extreme mood of anger will be more severe than shouting and in my case was slamming a door so hard the glass broke out of it or kicking something so hard that I was limping. This can look like a person is on steroids as the anger comes out in such a bad way that they cannot control themselves.

Extreme mood swings can also be crying uncontrollably and not being able to stop. This can be due to depression or pent up sadness that needs to come out. Extreme mood swings happen in waves and in a short space of time so a person experiencing these moods can be fine one minute then angry, then crying, laughing and back to being ok. This can happen quickly and be minutes apart rather than hours. Extreme mood swings can be a sign of any mental illness, so it may be useful to keep a diary of how you or a loved one are feeling or presenting themselves throughout the day. These mood swings being presented in someone with BPD may also come with paranoia and a person may constantly apologise or ask if they're annoying you.

Paranoia can manifest itself in how you feel about yourself and you worry that you are annoying or upsetting someone, but it can also mean that you are paranoid that you are seeing someone you know can't be there or you feel that you are being watched. This can show itself by a person constantly looking around them or feeling anxious. Paranoia is also linked to hallucinations and delusions which is another symptom of BPD.

7. Chronic feelings of emptiness

It is difficult to explain what it's like to feel empty inside if you haven't felt that way before. You sort of lose sight of who you are and feel like you have no emotions. You don't know where you belong in the world or what your purpose is. Feeling empty is feeling numb and you don't have any emotions in intense situations such as romance any you may self-harm to feel something. Chronic feelings of emptiness are linked to self- harm, substance misuse and suicide attempts as a person will do anything they can to feel something.

Self- harm, substance misuse and suicide attempts are usually not about wanting to die but about trying to feel something. You may feel that you do not have any emotions and can't feel anything and therefore you hurt yourself to feel physical pain because this reminds you that you are alive. Suicide attempts from feeling numb are often about trying to escape the feeling of being numb and empty that you can no longer live with. Dabbling in self- destructive behaviour may make you feel better for a little while or not at all but it is not satisfying, and you go back to feeling empty and lost.

Not feeling any emotions in a situation such as romance or a death is another form of feeling empty. A recent storyline on a soap was about a young man who was hearing voices and when he kissed a girl who he lived, he did not feel anything which frustrated him, so he stopped taking his medication. This is not a good thing to do, medication can curb your severe symptoms and should be taken as prescribed. I thought it was a very powerful storyline as it shows how people can feel nothing in a situation they ought to and so they get frustrated. Feeling empty when there is a death is also a good example as you want to feel angry and upset but cannot face reality. This can be caused by grief as well as being linked to BPD.

Feeling empty is also feeling detached from the world, like you don't belong everywhere and can dissociate. This means that you are behaving in a way that you don't remember because your brain has switched of. You can act in a nasty way and not remember what you have done. My experience of dissociating is when I self-harmed in a serious way such as burning myself or hurt other people, but I could not remember what I had done. It is hard to feel this way as you have to be told by someone else what you did or even speak to police because of an assault. I have been violent towards staff when I was in hospital which I am not proud of and I had to talk to police because I was not taking it seriously. The police will talk to you about an assault if they feel you know what you are doing but they generally understand that you are unwell. I have also spoken to police when I went missing or ran away and they were very useful in helping me to get the help I needed.

A person feeling empty will often feel sad and alone, like they do not matter, and no one cares. This is because they have masked their emotions and feel that the problem has temporarily gone away, and they can get on with their life. This is not a healthy way to live as you can feel alone and are prone to outbursts as your emotions try to escape your body. Not expressing your emotions means that they accumulate inside of you and you can become sensitive and irritable. Minor events can cause your emotions to explode out of you and you are now feeling real emotions which can be scary.

As human beings we have 3 responses to danger which are: fight, flight and freeze. The freeze response is often associated with a traumatic event and means that a person stopped feeling anything to protect themselves from a harmful situation or emotions. This can last longer than the dangerous situation and become more of a way of living. I had a traumatic childhood experience and as a result I became mentally unwell at 14. I have felt numb and empty, but it has got better since being in hospital as I was put on medication and learned mindfulness techniques to help me deal with any emotions.

I started to feel empty, that I noticed, at around 13 and I would often tell people that I did not know who I was or what my purpose was. I felt like I had to find myself which is linked to mirroring which I have previously spoken about. This is where you copy other people's mannerisms and habits in to find a part of yourself. I believe that I was living with BPD from a teenager but when you are still a child, therapists do not want to diagnose you or give you medication. At the age of 14 I was self- harming, attempting suicide, running away from home and having outbursts of emotions such as anger or sadness. I did not understand why I was behaving in this way but having been diagnosed with BPD I feel that I was experiencing symptoms of the illness.

Chronic emptiness is the opposite of feeling like your emotions are out of control and you do not know how to stop it. This is another symptom of BPD although it is not listed and means that an individual diagnosed with BPD can be prone to angry outbursts or crying at the littlest thing. I remember crying because the size of my dessert was too big, and I have thrown things across the room in a temper. You can experience emotional outbursts and feeling empty while you have BPD but not at the same time. The symptoms of BPD can change over time and mean that you are happy one minute and crying the next. This sounds a bit like bipolar and do not mean you have the other illness, but all the illnesses link together in some way, which makes it difficult to diagnose someone.

Feeling emotionally numb is not a conscious choice and can build up over time, with symptoms not being noticed until it has become 'normal'. You may have emotionally detached yourself from a terrible experience to not feel anything and instead of this going away when the abuse stops, you continue to feel numb in everyday life. Revealing your emotions may have led to rejection, abandonment or shame and therefore you learnt to stop showing your emotions until you no longer felt them. Abuse is a common cause of BPD as someone being abused or neglected would learn to deal with their emotions in a different way. Fear of abandonment and rejection is a big symptom of BPD and this is usually because of a person being mistreated in their childhood and they do not feel that they deserve love.

It is not until you decide to change your life and do something you will enjoy but is also useful that you learn how to feel whole again. The most significant milestone in my recovery was when I decided to study psychology with the open university so that I could help others but also so that I could understand myself better. I am going into year 3 of 6 and feel that my life has changed since starting my degree. It has given me a purpose and something to look forward to. I am studying part time which is why the degree is twice as long, but this works for me and allows me to work as well as study. My confidence has soured since I decided to study and got a job, which has helped me to pursue hobbies such as reading, writing and art. I attend an art group and sell canvas paintings in a local shop which has also helped boost my confidence. Everyone is different and will find different ways to help but the first step is asking for help.

8. Explosive anger

Explosive anger is a big part of BPD for me and it ties in with struggling to regulate emotions. Explosive anger can mean you get angry and upset over little things but can't control the feeling coming out. The worst time I had explosive anger was when I was sent back to a psychiatric hospital in England because I hadn't changed my GP to the one in Wales. It was not long after I had moved to my mum's and when I was sent back to England I had uncontrollable anger and was lashing out by punching walls and nearly getting into fights with other patients. I got very angry with another patient because she very loudly, so I could hear, asked a member of staff if she could put a can in their bin so that the self-harmers wouldn't get hold of it. I got angry and started shouting at her and walking towards her ready for a fight. There were staff telling her to leave and staff stopping me from moving towards her. I punched a wall in anger and had marks on my knuckles, I was given medication to help me calm down and sleep because I was struggling with sleep and the medication knocked me out. This was a nasty experience and I am not one for violence, but I couldn't control myself.

I get explosive anger more often than I would like because I get irritated and can't control myself, but it is mainly shouting and is usually directed towards my family. I have calmed down a lot since being on medication but before I was diagnosed I would lash out by trashing my boyfriend's room or hitting and kicking a friend. I do not like being angry, it is not a nice feeling, but it is hard to control when you get in a temper. I do not lash out and hurt people now but my poor mum usually get's the brunt of my rants and shouting. I have found that exercising has helped me to regulate my emotions and it is also good because I have made friends.

My anger is usually directed at myself and when I get angry and upset I self-harm. This is usually due to difficult circumstances that trigger me such as feeling unwanted, breaking up with a boyfriend or most recently due to death. I sadly lost my grandad last year and my dad stopped me from going to the funeral which upset me greatly and I ended up going back into hospital due to being unable to cope. While I was there I talked to staff about my feelings and it was explained to me that I was in the stage denial of grief. I thought I couldn't be in denial because I knew that my grandad was dead, but the nurse explained I was in denial of my emotions and not letting myself feel upset or angry. I cried a lot while in hospital but there was a lovely student nurse who brought me balloons and I wrote a letter to my grandad to send off into the sky. Unfortunately, it didn't work but I kept the letter.

Most recently, 5 months ago, my best friend in Wales unexpectantly died which distressed me. She was older than me at 46 but had been like a second mum to me since we met in hospital. She was very special to me and I looked forward to meeting up with her, so I was upset to hear of her death. She gave me a blanket to comfort me when I came out of hospital the time we were in together and I cuddled up to it the day I learnt she passed. I was happy to be able to go to her funeral, cry and say goodbye. She was a lovely person and I miss her every day. Before her funeral. I did try to commit suicide to be with her, but I saw how much it upset my mum and I haven't tried since. I am proud to say that I did not go into hospital when this hit me and have been out of hospital for 1 year 4 months. It was difficult when my friend passed but I had support to get me through.

Although I have been hospital free and using techniques such as art and exercise to help me cope, I still get outbursts of anger. I don't think that the anger will ever go away fully but I can control it. I learnt techniques such as mindfulness from a psychologist in the psychiatric hospital closest to me and that does help me but the most important thing to me is family and they keep me going. I now have 3 nieces and a nephew on the way and they give me strength to keep fighting. My eldest niece will be 2 at the end of this month (August) and I say that she saved my life because I was on such a downward spiral and didn't see a way out, but this little miracle gave me something to live for. She will always be special to me for that reason.

I mainly get explosions of anger when I feel like I am being rejected such as my mum not wanting to give me a hug or when I was irritable which usually happens when I am tired. These explosions of anger come out in the form of harsh words that can turn into an argument. I don't think, although they are supportive, that my family understand about my diagnosis or how to help me. That is one of the reasons for me writing this book, as well as to help other people and their families to understand. You also must take into consideration that other people have emotions too and so if you are both angry and upset then things can spiral quickly. It is better to talk about how your feelings if you can but the fact that the anger is explosive means it comes with no warning.

Explosive anger can come in physical forms as well such as someone punching or kicking walls or even people. My brother is diagnosed with intermittent explosive disorder, which is not commonly heard of, and he must take medication to help him too. It is difficult for my brother because his outbursts mean that he lashes out physically and he has been arrested for fighting. Since having his 2 girls and now having a son on the way, my brother has calmed down but he still get's irate and has got into a fight. This is not the best way to deal with people, talking is best, but it cannot be controlled on its own and I feel that more therapy should be available as medication is not enough on its own.

When I was first in a psychiatric hospital in England there was no therapy available, so my dad asked the Doctor if he could pay someone to come do sessions with me. The Doctor denied this and left me to get on with it. This is one of the reasons why my family decided I should live in Wales to get the right treatment. There is a better care system in Wales and when I have been in hospital here I have had therapy sessions where I talked through how to deal with my emotions, rather than what was triggering them. I found this very helpful, however, when you get out of hospital there is no therapy available except in groups. The best type of therapy for BPD is DBT, dialectical behaviour therapy, but this is not available in my area now. I have a care co Ordinator who I see every few weeks to talk but I feel that I do need therapy to help me deal with my past. I have been to an art group which helped, and I find exercise and writing helps but it is not the same as having the skills you need to help yourself when you are angry or upset.

Explosive anger is different for different people and can mean you lash out at yourself or others you care about. It is a big part of BPD as I explained in the introduction, it is hard for someone diagnosed to deal with their emotions. Talking is the most useful tool to have as it will help you to understand why you are angry and you can prevent it or lessen the intensity. It is useful for family members to understand that explosive anger is a symptom, but they need to talk to you about it and you can decide if there is help you need to ask for. It is also good for professionals to understand and not be quick to judge or label someone as a problem.

9. Feeling suspicious and out of touch with reality

I am glad that this symptom is at the end of the list because it needs to be talked about in detail and not over shadowed by the other symptoms, although they are all relevant. Feeling suspicious and out of touch with reality is an important symptom as it distinguishes Borderline from other personality disorders. Feeling suspicious is a common symptom of BPD as well as a person possibly displaying hallucinations and delusions. These symptoms are often associated with schizophrenia and therefore it is important to get a diagnosis before you start to speculate. BPD is different from schizophrenia because although you share symptoms such as hallucinations, you would not display the other symptoms associated with yourself.

Feeling suspicious is the more common symptom of the 3 when dealing with BPD and it can start suddenly or be linked to childhood trauma. Dealing with a trauma in your childhood such as abuse or neglect is what usually causes a person to develop BPD which is why professionals come up with this diagnosis when talking about dealing with trauma. Feeling suspicious can be thinking that someone is following you or you are going to get hurt.

My experience of feeling suspicious started when I was 16 and was in college. I had a bad experience associated with my mum when I was younger and at this time I was not in contact with her. Although she was living in Wales, I felt like she was everywhere and that she was following me. My biggest memory was phoning my then boyfriend in the night and he came to pick me up because I was so anxious, we went into Tesco and I was looking around, scared, as if I was on drugs, that was how he described it. It is very scary to feel unsafe and like you are being watched or followed and therefore it is important to talk to someone.

Hallucinations are also a part of BPD and are generally auditory, seeing things, but can be visual, seeing people or monsters. Hallucinations are normally voice's in your head that make you doubt yourself and tell you to hurt yourself or others. There is a different between hallucinations when you have a diagnosis of schizophrenia and one of BPD. People with BPD feel that the voices are inside their head rather than being able to hear them as if another person was talking to them.

My experience of hallucinations started of with seeing animals and children that would talk to me. These did not trouble me as they were nice, and I felt it was my duty to look after the children and play with them. The hallucinations then started to get more frequent and bad characters would come such as men who would stop me from leaving the house as I felt they were going to hurt me. I first started hallucinating when I was 19 but within about a year the characters had changed and led into delusions.

Delusions are when you believe something irrational such as that you are God, and no one can hurt you. This is an example of a patient I came across who believed this, and he stood in the middle of a train track because he believed he wouldn't be hurt. Delusions are generally linked to hallucinations and feeling suspicious and the mix can be terrifying for the person going through it but also their families. Medication is a key role in helping with these symptoms and the right dose will help someone's mind to settle back into a regular pattern.

My experience of delusions, as I partly explained in the introduction are that I believed I was a princess from another planet called Draymellone and that I had to die on Earth to be able to fight a battle in Draymellone. This delusion linked into my hallucinations as I believed that the children I saw were sent to me, so I could look after them while they were battling on my planet. This delusion progressed for months until I was trying to kill myself pretty much every day because I wanted to help 'my people'. It was particularly hard for my mum because when I was given help by being sectioned, I told a nurse that my mum wasn't my real mum and that I was fostered. This upset my mum because I was denying her as my family.

I was in a psychiatric hospital near home for 2 weeks and I was watched on a 1-1 by staff for those 2 weeks, constantly, because I was so determined to die. I was then moved to a psychiatric intensive care unit, or PICU, in North England and my mum was only able to visit me once. It was a very difficult and scary time as I felt no one understood me but after 2 weeks of medication I was sent back to the hospital near home. I was moved from a section 2 (can be detained for 4 weeks) to a section 3 (can be detained for up to 6 months) which distressed me greatly because I wanted to go home. However, I was only in hospital was another 2 weeks before I was allowed home. I was in hospital for my 22nd birthday although I was allowed out to spend the day and night with my family. After the 6 weeks of being in hospital and being on medication I felt more like myself again, although not fully. I was experiencing side effects such as feeling foggy and restless leg syndrome. I was later changed from risperidone to olanzapine during another hospital stay and the only side effect this gave me was weight gain.

I think in total I have been in hospital about 6 times, on about 7 different wards and I have lost count of the amount of times I have been admitted over the years. All the hospital stays helped me in some way, but it wasn't until I was given a diagnosis and put on medication that suited me, before I started to see a massive improvement and now I have been out of hospital for 1 year 4 months. I feel that this is an improvement because it is the longest I have been out of hospital for, the time before that being approximately a year and before that the record was 6 months. It is important to be given the right medication and therapy options to help you through the journey and most importantly to talk! If you are ever unfortunate enough to be in a psychiatric hospital then I would encourage you to talk to the doctors and nurses about how you feel and what will help, make the most of the time you have with professionals and make friends that understand you.

Conclusion

BPD is a very complex mental illness and it is categorised by many symptoms which I have tried my best to explain. I hope that you have found it useful to read about another person's experience of being diagnosed with a mental illness, whether you are diagnosed yourself, are a relative of someone diagnosed or even a professional. As you have read through the book BPD is categorised by emotions abnormalities such as fear, anxiety and rage but the main symptom that makes BPD is displaying signs of hallucinations and/ or delusions. It is difficult for a professional to diagnose any mental illness as they all link to each other in some way and even though you may be diagnosed with an illness such as BPD, that diagnosis can change to bipolar or schizophrenia later.

All mental illnesses are difficult to live with, whether you are dealing with depression, anxiety or something more complex, and it can be a scary place to be. ¼ of all people will be diagnosed with a mental illness in one given year and I am happy that it is more talked about and accepted in the 21st century than it was hundreds of years ago, yet there is still a lot of stigma surrounding mental illness. I find it upsetting when the older generation do not understand or when people say, 'I am so depressed today', like it is an illness you only feel for a day and then it is better. Mental illness often develops over the years and comes gradually rather than hits you suddenly.

There are several types of mental illness including eating disorders such as anorexia and bulimia, which I have battled with but will not go into in this book. My point is that there are different types of mental illness that display themselves in different ways but are all as scary as each other. You may mask your mental illness with food, smiles or laughter so that others are unaware of how you are feeling but this is not the best way to deal with mental illness, it is important to talk openly and honestly. I know this can be difficult because the first time I told my dad I was experiencing hallucinations he did not believe me but over time, he came around, and tried to help me the best he could.

I have been struggling with mental illness since I was 14 and I have recently turned 25 so only 10 years. I do not think that this is something that is ever going to go away with me, I feel that I am always going to have to fight to be strong but every day I am thankful that I am still alive and can enjoy my family and make new friends. I am open and honest with everyone about my mental illness but do try to avoid talking about it with someone new straight away, I want them to like me for who I am and not what I am diagnosed with. I am also currently doing a psychology degree to help me understand myself better as well as be able to help others. My main aim is to become an occupational therapist.

I feel it is important to get the message out there that no matter what you are diagnosed with or how far you are into the depths of your mental illness, it does get better, it does get easier and you can overcome it. I thought years ago that this was it for me, that I was going to be unwell forever or even dead but through talking to people, finding interests such as art that can help me and most recently exercise, I feel that my path has changed course and instead of giving in to my illness, I am fighting it every day to make sure that I am around for my family, to grow old and have a future.

Borderline Personality Disorder is a scary mental illness to have as you are labelled as emotional and psychotic but with the right support and medication you can overcome it and one day you may back to normal. That is what doctors like to say, that you will overcome it and live a normal life but personally I think it will always be a part of me and I am diagnosed with depression and psychosis separately. However, this may not be the case for you. I would encourage you to talk, find a hobby you love and even get back into education or work. You are diagnosed with BPD, you do not have it. BPD does not define you!